FRAYED OPUS FOR STRINGS & WIND INSTRUMENTS

FRAYED OPUS FOR STRINGS & WIND INSTRUMENTS

ULRIKKA S. GERNES

poems

TRANSLATED INTO ENGLISH BY
PER BRASK & PATRICK FRIESEN

Brick Books

Library and Archives Canada Cataloguing in Publication

Gernes, Ulrikka S.
[Flosset opus for strygere & blæsere. English]
Frayed opus for strings & wind instruments / by Ulrikka S. Gernes; translated into English from the Danish by Per Brask and Patrick Friesen.

Translation of: Flosset opus for strygere & blæsere.
Poems.
Issued in print and electronic formats.
ISBN 978-1-77131-376-6 (pbk.).—ISBN 978-1-77131-378-0 (pdf).—
ISBN 978-1-77131-377-3 (epub)

I. Brask, Per K., 1952–, translator II. Friesen, Patrick, 1946–, translator III. Title.
IV. Title: Flosset opus for strygere & blæsere. English.

PT8176.17.E72F5613 2015   839.811'74   C2014-907991-5
                                                   C2014-907992-3

First English edition, second printing (April 2016).
Originally published in Danish in 2012 as *Flosset Opus for Strygere & Blæsere* by Gyldendal Norsk Forlag.

We acknowledge the Canada Council for the Arts, the Government of Canada through the Canada Book Fund, and the Ontario Arts Council for their support of our publishing program. We also acknowledge the support of the Danish Arts Foundation for translation costs.

  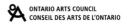

DANISH ARTS FOUNDATION

The author photo was taken by Christoffer Regild.
The book is set in Dante.
The cover was designed by Christopher Haanes.
Interior design and layout by Marijke Friesen.
Printed and bound by Sunville Printco Inc.

Brick Books
431 Boler Road, Box 20081
London, Ontario N6K 4G6

www.brickbooks.ca

TABLE OF CONTENTS

FOREWORD

In the late summer of 2012, Ulrikka Gernes sent Brask her new manuscript in a PDF about a month before the book was to be published in Denmark that fall. He was in Portland at the time visiting his eldest son and his family, enjoying the carnival atmosphere of a busy family with three young children. The title of Gernes's new book immediately seemed appropriate to the liveliness around him, a seesaw mixture of jubilant horns and occasional sad strings. He began reading it that evening and, besieged by images, knew pretty quickly that he wanted to translate this book, even before he'd completed reading it in hotel rooms on the road trip home. While en route he emailed Friesen to see if he'd be interested in working together on the translation. More than ten years earlier Friesen and Brask had edited and translated a collection of Gernes's poetry, an encounter all three found creatively satisfying.

Robert Frost is famously paraphrased as saying, "Poetry is what gets lost in translation." And that is certainly true if one thinks of translation as the transmission of the information delivered in one language into the equal and strictly corresponding information in another. That is, if that were even possible. But of course poetry is not information in that sense. It comes out of a life, somehow expresses or signals from that life, and as translators indeed we cannot re-live or re-express, re-signal that life. Fortunately a poem, as soon as it leaves the poet's pen and certainly once published, achieves an afterlife. So, while it may not have been created with a reader in mind, once out there, there they are, the readers, and they, hopefully, absorb the poem, play with it, use it on their own terms but always in relation to the poem, and the poem, though a ghost, lives again. In a way Frost, may as well have said, "Poetry is what gets lost in reading." Translations are readings of poems hopefully well absorbed and played with and though languages carry different echoes for their native speakers they are reciprocal, they can engage one another. Translation, in this view, is a way of engaging with a poem; this also gives an answer to the question of why translate poetry. Because it is a process that tickles the little grey cells on a variety of levels: thinking about context, text and subtext, as well as what resonances appear in its new instrumentation. And that is creatively satisfying when you start from poems that seem to address you in surprising ways. We had a good time with that the last time around. This time seemed again poised to deliver such satisfaction because Gernes was writing in a new way, had found a way of "talking" her life differently, to sound the years that had passed, the life that they were.

Brask sent Friesen some trial translations. Friesen worked on these, trying to make them resonate in this second language, and sent them back to Brask with suggestions and questions. Brask responded. Or, after Friesen's pass through, they would talk on the phone and go over possible versions. Then they'd send it all to Gernes who, with a decent command of English herself, would comment, point out misreadings, make suggestions and changes. Friesen and Brask would confer, accept Gernes's changes or make additional changes, and send the manuscript back to Gernes. Eventually Gernes approved and work was completed. That was the process in brief.

It is in the several crossings back and forth between languages that the essence of translation resides. The literal is a kind of necessary platform upon which the transitions perform. Always they reference literal meaning, though literal meaning is itself an approximation. Questions of sound, of the varying resonances of images in the different languages, are constantly being asked. Translation is, in this way, a process of questions that can be answered fully sometimes, but often only partially much of the time. Perhaps, in the end, poetry is what is gained in questions and approximation.

Patrick Friesen and Per Brask, July 2014

FRAYED OPUS FOR STRINGS
& WIND INSTRUMENTS

A FRAYED OPUS FOR STRINGS
and wind instruments
and a lit bicycle shed
in the backyard; all that desire
constrained in shuddering
apartment blocks from where
my mind wanders
on daylong steep mountain paths
only to curl up
against your sleeping back
on a bespoken globe.

NIGHT-BLACK SILVER, JANUARY'S LUMINOUS
morning-darkness leaves behind its blacking,
rubbing off on everything I touch.
It could be worse, it could
always be worse, but could it
be better? No, never better than
this moment, it's perfect, it'll never
come back. The child sleeps,
the cat plays with its tail, traffic
sighs past on Falkoner Allé. I jot this down
in the margin of the newspaper, drink
a cup of tea, somewhere someone
opens a book, the year has just begun,
and life, the late dawn sneaks in,
polishes the dark spots clean.

THE IMAGE OF THE RIVER FILLS MOST OF THE PICTURE,
the way the runoff from the hinterland, according
to the season, gradually makes it spread into
the valley. Close to the riverbank the water is clear,
flowing over rocks overgrown with waving plants,
quenching the thirst of many living creatures
and offering the flora a near bombastic lushness.
Here the river is shallow with only a weak current,
gathering lazily outside of the rainy season as though
preparing for a leap it needs time to ready. Like a
river valley in a highland jungle, where the water
is far from its source and still further from the ocean.
That I, here at this precise riverbank, marry the owner
of a sports apparel company, doesn't take up nearly
as much space in the dream. The fact that I'm happy
is the least of it all.

FEBRUARY'S HEART THUMPS TO TAKE THE CHILL
off the pulse, the path to the Netto supermarket
crosses thawing wastelands covered
with bottle caps and cigarette butts;
a fallow field in my chest begs
for an advance, a reprieve, for mercy,
begs for everything that can be begged for,
a straw, even the shortest, the tiniest sprout,
at the cash register beneath florescent tubes;
one hundred in cash back please, well then, just
the amount; I gather myself, stack
and pack, stomp back home through
an eternal Tuesday's endless afternoon;
my lips sealed around a sentence
from your mouth, uttered by mine;
and the sparrows sparkle diamonds in a flock
beneath the beech hedge's leathery leaves
in the raw, wool-grey dusk
in the suburb of the Moon.

K WAS SUPPOSED TO COME WITH THE KEY, I WAS
to wait outside the gate. I arrived on time,
the time we had agreed on and waited, as agreed,
outside the gate. I waited a long time, waited
and waited, waited a very long time. I stood
next to the security guard from Securitas, who also
stood outside the gate. I waited, the security guard
from Securitas just stood there, he wasn't waiting,
it was his job to stand there, he didn't take
any breaks, he just stood there, keeping an eye
on what he was supposed to keep an eye on. K
didn't show up. I waited. When the security guard
from Securitas finished his shift I went home
with him, sat down across from him at the kitchen
table, ate spicy meatballs on rice, summer cabbage
followed by green tea and mango from Brazil.
In the night he laid his human hand between
my shoulder blades before we both stumbled
across the threshold into a brand new now.

SPARKS SLEEP IN FLINT AND I, AMORPHOUS, AM THE ANSWER
should anyone ask. I won't even pretend to symmetry.
You may easily let your finger run along the mountain
chain of my spine, follow the stream through the landscape,
look me up in Jurassic layers. I linger and let myself be led;
perhaps it's to do with age; I have no need for extremes,
but for quiet, as if the material is not yet tamed; raw
and the size of a fist, I keep my heart on a tight leash,
knowing all too well its subversive acts and that single
beat that exposes the fracture in the light of a firestorm.

BARELY FIVE MINUTES LATER WE'VE MOVED INTO
a seven-bedroom apartment on Rosenborggade
with exposed collar beams and rafters
of Pomeranian pine which make the whole construction
visible for anyone to see; the dimensions of a brick
are made to fit a man's hand, door handles and hasps,
fleeting caresses, crisp stucco, look, it matches
my dress; tightly veined wooden floors sated with resin,
those eye-like knots have dried their tears long ago
and all the details about piping and drainage systems
that you have no desire to know are loosing themselves
in the whoosh of an extinct forest, a distant sigh
from Galicia's giant trees flows through the rooms;
I do believe I perceive animal paths twisting through
the thicket of our kisses, wondering whether you too
sense those shadows passing by, shaggy, vigilant,
but with no hesitation about direction or aim,
the scent tears slightly in my nostrils;
you're right: there's more between heaven and earth
than flesh and blood, and I, who never favoured
timber frame, am able all at once to gloss over
your escapades; the raft that carries me across
the rapids is built of longing; no stronger timber
exists and it floats just as easily as it burns.

A MICROSCOPIC SHIFT IN THE AIR MOLECULES
shoots the moment out of the chain of moments;
it trembles in the air, an abrupt happiness; the coins
leave your palms, shiny, clean, cool; in exchange
for bread, parsley, a bag of apples, that you
pass to me without blinking, in one single
sliding extension of yourself; our bodies
yielding, formed by each other's wind
and ocean; I wave eelgrass in your undercurrent,
your glittering school quivers silvery in mine
in the crowd around us and no one sees it,
except for the surveillance camera's fish eye
below the cornice that catches a grey-toned
screen picture of a man and a woman, caught
in the act from an oblique, bending angle
on a Saturday morning at the market.

NOT A SINGLE LEAF EXISTS ON A SINGLE
tree that doesn't turn in the wind to reveal
an image of your face, not a single tree exists
on a single globe that doesn't grow wildly,
wonderfully from your sleeping breath,
not a single freckle exists on your only
back that doesn't have a sister star afar;
your luminous skin is connected to the sky
above my night, and this moment, wedged in.

RUSHING FORWARD BELOW UNDULATING ARCHES
in a hurricane of composure, having to catch
capitals, Ionic, Doric, Corinthian, as they fall
like ripe fruit into my arms. Not even columns
of marble are able to offer support, they tumble
like pins when the hoofbeats of contractions drum
quakes into the body's ground, a gathering of earthly
arrival. *Ha!* It's up to me and it's now! to build
the pyramids, the Suez Canal, the Great Wall of China,
all by myself and alone, wrenching my pod inside out,
wresting a heart from my heart. The force; pushed
in a different direction it would stop the Earth's rotation,
shift the globe's axis, it would shoot rockets to the Moon
and further still, to the edge of eternity, that would be
far easier, but there is no lowest part of the fence here,
no place to jump. Pulling myself, helpless, split,
through a frayed thicket of female form fixed
in reproduction's violence and incomprehensible
tenderness, I cling to the idea of a message in a bottle,
a straw, an island; evening and night, dawn, morning
and day, hours and still more hours. Blood-heavy swells
rumble against the breakers over oyster banks, a nervous
needle draws tops and troughs on the strip of life, layer
upon layer of mother of pearl rolls around a living pulse,
stretched to the bursting point in the eye of the storm,
before the steel is set, the shell wrenched open and *you*
are lifted, blood dripping, from the ocean's foaming
wound-edges into the light here.

I RETRIEVE THE LETTERS FROM THE BOX
at the bottom of the closet; it's been
a while, but now the time is ripe.
I wash them, dry, buff and polish
vowels, consonants; I put the kettle on
and make a cup of tea from the green banks
of the Brahmaputra River, black Assam,
sipping it standing by the window while
I watch the wood pigeons swaying heavily
on the branches of the maple tree. Then I
check them one by one for chips and cracks,
fix them up the best I can; some are more
tarnished than others, there's no mistaking
the wear and tear of age, the fissures
can't be mended, but they all add
to the impression of experience, patina,
a touch of nostalgic charm that I hope
will please; the rustic strain. When finally
I think the result cannot get any
better, I put them together
and hand them to you.

IN THE BEAM FROM THE TAXI'S HEADLIGHTS
I see my silhouette climb the stairs.
I put out my hand, outlining
a precise limit, unguarded—
my silhouette, a broken line flickering
around the scene of the crime
where a dream lies barely buried.
In the beam from the taxi's headlights
I see the silhouette insert the key
deep into my heart, twisting the metal
around, and open up. Little by little
the eyes adjust to the dark.

I BRING A LARGE BUNCH WITH ME BACK HOME
hiding the wound behind the bouquet; lilies,
blind, sleeping; I put them in a vase
on the table, they stand on stiff stems
fumbling in the air, unknowing. In the early
hours, a faint crackle in the room; membranes
break, wake up. Their blindness but a dream.
Eyes of darkness, of the world, so much visibility!
From the vase on the table they whisper yellow,
waiting for me to answer, for me to tell
all that happened in the meantime.
They stare unbelieving and stay silent.

WHO WOULD HAVE THOUGHT THAT CHESTS
of drawers could suddenly turn brittle and crisp,
no longer able to hold the weight of a letter,
that a sparkling strand of hair whirled in
beneath the radiator would be a fire hazard,
a reason for evacuation, that mirrors could
be emptied of features, beds lose their way,
a body razed to wasteland because of a scent.
I have arranged a life in the void you left
behind when you shut the attic window
behind you, jumped and disappeared.
I float here, weightless, transparent, afoul
of the law. When I look up I don't know
whether it's the stars or my eyes that glitter
from what no one would have thought.

THE CALL OF THE KNIFE-GRINDER IN THE ALLEY AT DAWN, THE KNIVES
answering dully from the drawer, a gecko laughing from the ceiling,
sweat sticks day to night, skin to skin, Hong Kong;
clouds saddle up over the islands in the South China Sea,
hurling runaway horses against the city, the typhoon flings
its whirling mane anti-clockwise, turns back time
and my thought; your hand melting into my hip.

THE DECISIVE MOMENT, THE DECISIVE
place? We grew quiet, suddenly
unable to share, uncertain whether
it was the same thought
that twisted through the both of us
and now much later I can't tell
whether the image is haunting
you too: the riverboat at dawn
as if seen from the far bank,
seeing it hover on an arch of sky,
a belt of liquid silver, seeing it shift
softly in a whirlpool's dance, seeing us
there on the deck, seeing us seeing *them*—
We embarked from Mandalay bound
for Pagan. It was still dark,
that dark which souls travel in
when forever or in dreams they depart
their shells. But then dawn broke;
we were living, animated bodies
and the landscape unfolded
its fan below a fine, golden mist,
blessed, as on the day of creation.
They were by themselves on the 1st class
deck, we shared 2nd class with crowds
of locals and their odd assortment
of baggage, we couldn't afford such
luxury, not even here in the 3rd world.
They were twenty to thirty years ahead,
but we...I glanced at you to check
if you were also looking and you
were. Even their clothes. Those
kind of clothes we'll be wearing in

twenty to thirty years, right? Also
the way they moved, confidentially
addressing each other, a deep
love's mirroring of movements.
They breathed through each other,
completed each other's sentences,
knew every tiny shift of mood,
the smallest muscle contraction,
they lived as one inside each other.
Did they see us? Did they see themselves
in us, knowing all that had happened,
would happen in the meantime, that we
would, that they would lose one another,
live skewered, awkward lives continents
apart, be inconceivably happy, yes,
in glimpses, though mostly inconceivably
unhappy in a safe, everyday humdrum
way, continually changing addresses,
having children, infections and new
in-laws against all reason, and then
perhaps at some point in time
lean against the railing of a riverboat
on Irrawaddy, as if nothing . . . I write
this approximately halfway, my hand
will not finish the sentence, will
not lift from the paper, while
the boat silently glides past
in the morning darkness, dawn
after dawn after dawn—

THE CHESTNUT TREES ARE BLOOMING ALONG
the lakes every year at this time reminding
me of the affair we never had despite
the many small furry attempts that
walked the tightrope between our glances.
The light from chestnut flowers or is it
the shine of your pale-soft face that throws
an invisible shuttle back and forth, weaving
you still tighter into the threads of my mind
every year at this time along the lakes' mirrors,
where you appear behind my shoulder and
graze my neck, until again you withdraw into
your grave in the shade of the chestnut trees.

I HAVE TO FIND F. I DON'T KNOW WHY AND I DON'T KNOW
where, but if I find F I'll get the answer to an important
question. I don't know the question, but at some
point I'll be told. It's something to do with an
envelope. And a parrot feather. I'm in London.
I have a photo of an English row house, the kind of house
there are a million of in London. I have no address.
I only know that it's in London and that F is in the house
in the photo. I must find that house. I have two large
suitcases that are very heavy. In addition I have a rucksack
on my back. It too is heavy. I can barely carry my luggage.
I also have a dog. A small, black and white dog which is
very lively. I have it on a leash but it constantly runs
away from me. Its name is Ziggy. I call and call after it.
It leaps and jumps and barks. It's impossible to control it.
We walk through dark, narrow passages and alleys that
dead-end and we have to walk back. It seems hopeless,
but I mustn't give up. I yell and yell after the dog that
constantly skips away from me. In my pocket I have
the photo of the house, I have to stop continually, put
the suitcases down, take the photo from my pocket
and compare the house in the photo with the houses
we pass. In this way seventeen years go by.

I WRITE THIS ON THE BACK OF A TURQUOISE-BLUE
coastline, make an X, wishing you were here,
where my body has washed ashore. I'm with you
as a thought this morning. The letter slot
clangs, you bend down, pick up the picture from
the doormat, unshaven, in a bathrobe; tilting your
head you wonder at the colour of the ocean,
an upside-down sky, the clarity of the water,
as though it were impossible to drown.

ON THE TABLE IN THE ROOM IN THE DARK
house lies the book you didn't know
you were looking for, opened to the page
with the poem about solace you didn't know
you needed; at first the letters,
then the words, little by little
the lines disappear as you read them
in the light of the faint dawn that trickles in
between the venetians' dusty
slats and unites you with someone
you didn't know you are.

STRUGGLING THROUGH SLEET IN ORDER TO
catch it, but the doors shut, the bus moves
heavily out of the curb's slush, turns
into the traffic of Nørre Allé with its silent
cargo of bodies in damp coats, oozing
the warmth of wool, dark humanity; and there,
from behind a window half-covered with steam,
approximately in the middle of the carriage,
I watch myself standing on the sidewalk,
gasping for air as the bus disappears into a row
of heavy vehicles in the bottomless winter dusk
on the globe's northern hemisphere.

ODD HOW YOU ARE IN MY THOUGHTS
these days, how you sneak through
crevices I didn't know were there.
Has something happened? Are you okay?
Why are you rising from the deep,
is something going on, something brewing
down there? I thought I had learned
to stay on the surface, to skate
or something that looks like skating, but then
you look up at me through the ice. Aren't you
a little pale or is it the dark background
that does it? Maybe it's just the angle
that seems troubling or because
your mouth opens and closes
like a fish, and it's impossible to hear
what you are saying, if you are saying
anything, but your lips . . . and of all
the first kisses I've ever had, it's only
yours that I recall; the suction,
the sinking, the vanishing and all
that suddenly no longer existed.

VIA VENETO. I WRITE TO YOU ON THE HOTEL STATIONERY
with the hotel pen; the establishment has seen better
days, the grey-scale of *La Dolce Vita*; I didn't know that time
means so much until I came here; I mean, I didn't know
that time means so little here in the eternal city and still
it's been a long while since anyone said, all roads lead etc.,
but when you lift your eyes from the poem on page 24,
you are here; the sirens howl, columns of dust and oblivion,
the heat strikes as a shock, everyone is busy; you ask, what
does time mean? It's been a long time since anyone asked
for Salvatore Quasimodo; there's a certain confusion about
the monuments, a Roman soldier is smoking a Marlboro
on the Spanish Steps; under the vault of the heavens
above the Colosseum a seagull and a crow fight a furious
gladiator fight, screams, feathers, screams, over a crust
of bread; I'm wearing my blue dress, the pleated one
that folds like the marble folds on the statues, like time
folds, like the city loses itself in its folds, disappears, regains
its senses in yet another breathtaking piazza, the poem
will never be finished; Rome, by definition, I roam around,
scratch a stanza there, a word here, a letter, a piece
of a letter, an insignificant oral sound; the air,
as you said, writes the poem itself; I have to catch it
in a breath, here it is: not much to write home about;
I roll up the sheet of paper, put it in a bottle, send it off
in the Tiber, shadow bridge upon shadow bridge,
the Mediterranean will take care of the rest;
may my letter find you in good health;
life is short, write soon, yours, U.

PRAGUE 1991. I HAD SEEN HER STANDING OUTSIDE THE CAFÉ
for a long time, seen her check her watch, look first
in one direction then in the other, seen her walk a little
back and forth, how her back had swayed under her coat,
her small neck agitations; she was slim, her coat well fitted,
dark-blonde hair in a short pageboy cut. Over the edge
of the newspaper my thoughts had touched upon the reasons
for her waiting; the lover who didn't show up and why, but
only superficially in the way we let ourselves be entertained
by the fates of others, as long as they don't get entangled
into our own. It had started to rain, just a little, a drizzly
spring rain, it didn't matter, she continued to wait, as if
waiting were a task that was required of her and that she
fulfilled while carefully suppressing a growing desperation,
pulling her coat closer to her body. I had browsed further,
read headlines, looked at pictures, gotten shades of ink
on my fingertips. By the time I had peered again over
the edge she was staring into the café. I had thought that
it must have been difficult to see anything but one's own
mirror image, the way glass reflects when what's on the other
side is dark and diffuse, as with train windows at night
when the landscape rushes by and still all you can see
is your own face, pale in the glass. Maybe she was looking
at herself. I had returned to the article in the *Herald Tribune*,
something about Nagorno-Karabakh, an objective
description of a tense situation, fittingly distant so as
not to be pressing. I drank the last sip of coffee; it had
turned lukewarm and intensely sweet from the bit
of sugar cube that hadn't been completely dissolved
when the coffee was still hot; for a moment I had considered
ordering another cup whenever the waiter next came by,

but there were many customers in the café in that early
afternoon, lively groups, enclaves of solitary newspaper
readers and couples sitting close, conversing quietly;
the waiter was busy, and then I had the sense of being
watched, that eyes were seeking me out, were resting
upon me, drilling into me, very near, and I looked up.
Are you Anne Franklin? She asked holding my gaze
in those few seconds that went by before the room
exploded in chalk-white light. Since then I have
been standing in the subway, singing to passersby
and no one knows my name.

YOU ONLY LOVE ME WHEN I SMOKE;

I love a blue apple tree.

THE ROAD IS LONG AND WHO KNOWS WHAT AWAITS?
With a little luck a town with a guest house, where
perhaps you can get the corner room. A bed, a sink,
a closet you'll never open. There's no reason
to unpack. Soon you'll likely be on your way again,
or never, but be prepared! In the town you can walk
about as though you were waiting for something,
a message, a stamp on an important document or better
weather, and just whiling away time. Perhaps you meet
someone and have a couple of children or an indelible
memory. The shift is a gesture that gives you room
to play. And you stop in front of a shop window after
closing time and you imagine yourself dressed up
in the red dress, the strapless one. Reckless, you think,
and envisage the life that comes with it, quite easily.
All things considered you might as well be someone else,
present yourself as Dorte or Agnes, maybe a foreign
name, Florentina, and put on an accent no one is really
able to place. A sex change, but then the ploy would
belong in a different category. It is dusk, some autumn
or other; collars turned up, rain against the wind, people
almost pass by themselves, almost like walking coats,
no one's glances turn you inside out, you can remain
openly invisible as whoever you are. Just for today.
It provides a certain calm. As though, after all, it
doesn't mean so much. To love. To be loved. You
enroll in a course in astronomy and develop a much
closer relationship with the stars, you even get attached
to a particular constellation and at long last you quit
smoking. In a box of odds and ends at the second-hand
shop you find your first kiss, somewhat faded, among

handkerchiefs, old coins and oil lamps. Thoughtfully,
you let it slide back and forth between your hands. Has
it really been that long and still it's not a real antiquity yet?
The radio announcer says that flies evolved from crayfish.
For a moment desperation runs free; what will happen
to you? Luckily it soon passes and you turn around
corners into quiet neighbourhoods. Here all your old
boyfriends live. You recognize the names on the clattering
mail slots, but no one knows any longer which key fits
the lock to which door or exactly what it is that's
drowning in the flash of light behind the glossy surface
that always shuts hurriedly again and that strange music
just before the curtain comes down. Faces whirl up confetti
along the sidewalk, blink and change with glittering eyes,
but what happened to the letters with all that desire
and eagerness, flowing in ink and blood toward an
assumed fate? That moment. The decisive one. When
it happened. And didn't happen. Or something else.
You move the furniture around, get new curtains,
grey where your hair parts and put a lid on a few
useful experiences. Someone or other starts laughing
someplace, sounds like a hyena. Jackals have longer
ears, don't they? One thing always leads to the next
and you ask yourself whether you could have avoided
this, if only one thing or the other. Or if not. Once
you can handle the clutch, it's easy enough to drive.
It's all about coordination. You can safely accelerate.
The definition of a bird is not wings, but feathers.
Absent-mindedly you study your nails, rims
of dirt, yet again you have been messing about

down there. He who digs a grave and so on.
The floors slide in slow motion. Even when you
know your preconditions, the credits rolling
on the inside of the eyelids, the premonition always
stops the moment before the accident happens.
It's not speed that kills, but what you run into.

IN THE THICKET OF POSSIBILITIES I CHOOSE THE CONTINENTAL
shelf as my ford, find foothold, take off, firmly determined
to fall in with the spirit of the place, but in vain; I tumble
flopping through the mesh in the net; in the broom closet I have
the company of some rat-like creatures, one of them maintains
it has found the Northwest Passage, possibly just a polite excuse
to make conversation; later on, none of us have been there before,
the dinner party continues and the guests are served baked apples
with licorice meringue, my dinner partner is missing the tip
of his left thumb, I pretend I haven't noticed a thing, fall
in love with lightning speed the moment the guard takes
a nap at the floodgate, always this desire to fill a void, to fit
my body into the shape of someone else's solitude, and the
answers whirring in the air search for questions far too close
to the candles' nervous flames; tonight all men are my husband,
all women his wife, I'm no one's daughter, no one's sister,
no one's mother, anyone can see that my face has travelled, air
hostess, I reply, when anyone queries, I feel dizzy and leave
early, the long haul to Shanghai my excuse.

ALL NIGHT LONG I PARTICIPATE IN A QUIZ SHOW, WAKE UP
before it airs, *live*, exhausted as if having just run
a marathon I must yet again reconsider
my life, moored to the rainbow; a little later
I'm on the train to Herlev as though that's the solution;
the woman in the seat across from mine speaks Uzbek
loudly into her cellphone; outside the station an older
couple is handing out *The Watchtower*, for free they say
and refuse to take my coin; concrete, graffiti, a heavy
puff of hawthorn, I kick a fir cone quite a ways
down Violinvej, I'm travelling through space,
Earth's rules of play appear to me immensely
provincial, especially regulations concerning
parking; my vessel has been confiscated, and I'm
lost without you.

THIS EVENING IS MY EVENING, SHE SAID, HE SAYS, THIS EVENING
you must do all that I say, she said, he says. And she asked
him to choose the music, the music that is closest to eternity,
Handel, among others. Then he turned over the records
and he was gentle, because that's how he was, like now,
and that's how I'll remember him, a hint of impossible love.
There were champagne and oysters, he says, and tiny, pale
amaretti macaroons, flown in from Rome, miraculously
not a single one was broken until they cracked between
tongue and palate and filled the mouth with a bitter sweetness,
like the one that fills me now, and from below the window
they could hear her husband walking back and forth, while
she opened her robe and commanded him to touch
the lumps. They are still there in the hands he reaches
across the café table, now twenty-seven years later, in a city
whose name we will both shortly have forgotten.

AN INTERGALACTIC COLLISION OF LIGHTS, SOUNDS
and smells chases the thoughts backwards down the stairs
along the garden path with the broken stones
out through a rusty metal gate at the end of the wall
in order to get back to the precise wording
of a carelessly dropped remark that so many
years later, now, makes me turn left instead
of turning right and pulls me head over heels, the pulse
screeching with adrenalin, through a fusty arcade
and out into the sun-shrill piazza in the midday heat
where crickets saw and file at the monument to silence
and no one could imagine it humanly possible to do
any kind of physical work in this heat wave
but the swaying back of a half-naked youth
carrying something heavy past an open window
quickly disappearing into the darkness of the back room
hurtles my heart down into the bottomless black-blue gorge
over the entrance of which your name hangs, dangling.

REMEMBER, LONGING DOESN'T DIMINISH OVER THE YEARS,
rather it grows, he says, and I know that the allusion
isn't directed at me as we both grow quiet at the sight
of tradesmen with naked torsos in the midday heat
in the square in front of the church, both of us marvelling
at a neat pattern of body hair across a chest, down along
the navel, the play of muscles in the network of drops
of sweat, the bird-like flight of an upper lip's arch; arms, hands,
the bend in the neck and its toss, to be a man, to be a man,
to be a woman, love knows no age and no gender,
love is a window, and maybe it's because the air shimmers
short of breath from heat, death and lavender
that all at once I wish for nothing else but for him
to hold me on a discarded mattress in the parking lot beneath
the Tears of St. Lawrence, he can fuck me in the ass, if he wants,
for a moment the both of us can abandon who we are.

DOGGER BANK, ALL THAT JUNK, WORDS
from childhood's radio are turned on. Clutter.
The brain's chemistry, perhaps; the marine forecast,
but why now, exactly this morning, March,
overcast, plus eight degrees Celsius; hungover,
I have a bath. Under the shower my soapy hand
touches an unknown face beneath the slippery foam,
her delicate features not mine at all; her thoughts
rummage in my head in a language I don't know;
she stands on a ghat in the Ganges, water up to her waist,
washing away her sins, blessing herself; Varanasi, the pyres;
but would I really wish myself out of the cycle of rebirth,
no longer hold an insignificant hope of yet another
life as a weevil, a mite, the neighbour's wire-haired
dachshund, anything just to stay. Right. Here.
I remove my hand, turn my face against
the water jets; on the floor above,
Chopin rolls across the floorboards
gathering gold dust into a ball of mercury.

ON H. C. ANDERSEN BOULEVARD DURING RUSH HOUR
around five o'clock I'm a speck of stardust on a bicycle
wrapped in my life's nanosecond, my life's nanosecond,
my life's nanosecond and this poem that doesn't really
fit in anywhere either, and I have already wasted an infinitely
immeasurable fraction of the light intended for me, as I just
manage to glimpse the wing tip of a herring gull tear
a white cut into the air above Langebro, a tear in the blue
and there you are and there's my daughter, the strings, the wind
instruments, a tiny stage and a fragile ship ascending on
the waving pillar of smoke from a cigarette someone
tosses and butts right now under the heel against a flagstone
in the universe and a bleeding cut on the lip screams,
have I loved, have I loved, have I loved enough.

ALONG NIGHT'S SLIPPERY SLOPE, SHINY STEEL
tracks, you suddenly push in here, inscrutable,
round among sharp edges with your offbeat hairstyle,
the dark moons of your eyes, a smile wistful for lipstick
and that run in your stockings that moves higher
and higher up your thigh announcing a dubious dawn
at the end of this, right now you merely sense it as a vague
distress on the outskirts of your heart; and I want to wrap
my arm around your shoulders, chit-chat you back into history,
around the corner, down the street and up the stairs, put
the key in the door and with almost unnoticeable movements
open and close cupboards and drawers, the hiss of the gas element
the clink of metal against glass; everything but a distant hum
from the cosmos that drowns out the minute click when the lock
shuts behind me and you float swaddled in a veil of sleep,
unhurt, loved and under the influence of warm milk
and honey.

EXACTLY WHAT I WAS MEANT TO PICK UP
I still don't know, but I came back
with gelatin. How long have I stood
by the window? The clouds are building up
over the rooftops; the rooftops become the horizon
here on the 3rd floor. They keep up appearances,
or rather: the transformation happens so slowly
that it's almost unnoticeable. Perhaps
because I start thinking about something
else. Somewhere between two days and two
years. Left. To live. You can build a world,
tear it down again, you can let go, let
the transformation happen; as a cloud let
yourself be led by the wind over
the rooftops, the horizon; passing by
the 3rd floor window.

THE HEADLINES SHOUT ABOUT ABUSED CHILDREN AND SACKED
TV hosts as I'm on my bike heading toward Vanløse, where
my father grew up, in order to get some tablecloths pressed
at the Star Dry Cleaners on Ålekistevej 103. On my way back
I buy a coat in the Salvation Army shop at Jydeholmen
for 75 kroner. Black wool. The salesperson complains
about her mother who hasn't gotten out of bed yet and it's past
one o'clock, but now for sure I'll be able to keep warm.
The light transforms the road into milk. I hold a tension
in my chest when I pass the gate to the house where you lived
toward the end, I see you before me on your way from the shop
with the bottle in your hand. The universe consists for the most
part of dark matter, perhaps that's what makes the stars light up.
At Finsensvej I stop and buy a smoked mackerel, some goat cheese
and marzipan from Lübeck. In front of the supermarket a large
shaggy dog is waiting, at home the local paper and the first lines
of a poem. Would it have made any difference had we known
it was toward the end?
Light is still travelling.

SKINNY PEOPLE ARE MORE NAKED, YOU SAID,
shy from seeing me undressed, posed
on the bench, I had to close my eyes, wasn't allowed
to look at you when you let my raw body float
across the paper, as if you cried me out into abstract
watercolour. It's not until much later that the subject
dissolves, in the shower, when I suddenly realize
the dead have forgotten us, that's the boundary,
and I still remember you, wild, detailed, alive;
the shock bounces back on me; you are gone, you
have forgotten my watercolour which is running
down the drain; a drop of gasoline shimmering
in the wet asphalt as you arch
a fat rainbow over the city.

YOU LEFT ME A THREE-ARMED CANDELABRUM
made of silver and a one-person board game.
I put up the pieces, my fingertips slip the smooth
ivory shapes into the holes in the board's
worn intarsia making my first a predictable
move. I consider a cynical strategy, to clear the field
from end to end. Or, should I rather surrender myself
to chance? The game takes out one piece and yet
another. That's the point of the game. The taken
pieces add to the pile next to the board, the losses
mount with the years in anyone's life. The point here is
to have as few pieces left as possible. Only one is best.
A single one. You. And here I am, one, single, alone;
a pile of dead pieces on the side. The candles flutter,
shadows flicker in the room, seeking the dark holes
to rise up in neat rows and start over.

IT'S AS THOUGH YOU WERE JUST HERE;
the door stands ajar, the wind lifts nearly
unnoticeably a sheet of paper from the table.
Senses ask the consciousness for advice.
No, I'm not really in despair,
it's just a dying forest
that tumbles down through me.

THE SNAKE RATTLES AMONG THE DRY LEAVES
at the bottom of the garden, is it a sigh,
a hiss? My sandaled feet, bare ankles,
paper skin inscribed with burst vessels,
read: naked legs and up higher, lightning's
bite; you rush within me, poisonous sweetness.
Wedded is wedded, poison to poison, separated
again, but this has forever hooked on to me,
twisting its scaled body within my body,
gnawing salt from a shoulder, freckles from
an underarm; on the tip of its left fang
my heart pulses, thumping your naked name.

NO MORE NOW. EVEN FEAR HAS FEAR. EVEN OF ITSELF.
I refuse to be lonely. No longer. It's enough now.
Language contradicts itself, constantly producing
additions, disclaimers and footnotes. And the body
never gets ready, nails grow out, and hair, in the strangest
places. Here the mountainside is black with lemons.
At the very moment I rest within my contour a dam
breaks. Maybe there's a connection. I am someone
who . . . bounded by skin, is alone. I say it again, as loud
as I can: not another word! Maybe everything is connected.
Several thousand kilometers away you move your hand.
And here everything is instantly flooded.

I DRAG THE DEPTHS OF A LIFE FOR A SINGLE
glimpse of a face; the childhood is waiting,
forever unfinished and just for us; poppies
sway in the wind in a wasteland in the galaxy;
you brush past me, light years away in the night.
Faces flash, shift, blink off, layer upon layer
of one and the same, you too carry these features
of being human, making you seen in the crowd,
eyes into the soul, a dream barely dreamt,
a failed imprint of a finger; a childhood
is all we get, forever unfinished and just
for us; the childhood before we meet again.

I CLIP FEAR OF DEATH ONTO THE UPPER
right corner of a note from the 3rd floor.
If everything goes wrong, I can always
run down to the corner shop. The sound
from the dishwasher in the background
generates a sensation of activity, but what
is my contribution to the creation of value
in society? Probably not this poem.
Maybe another one, some other time,
a kind of continuation. *In the choir*
of rain every drop sings. From the corner
of my eye I see the four walls move closer.
In the choir of rain every word sings.
I reach my hand out through the window
toward that specific segment of humanity
which begins and ends with you.

THAT I HAVE AN ATONAL ABRUPT RELATIONSHIP
with time has nothing to do with the fact that I don't
sleep at night, but rather that night has rolled
itself up into a warm ball of fur behind my
closed eyes' closed eyes and for that reason
I have difficulty balancing on the timeline; I fall
in pieces, stumble into black holes, entwined
in teenage years, the web of menopause; a forever
ancient sorrowful schoolgirl plays hooky within me
to sit out maths on the bench by the river
and keep an eye on someone who walks by many
years before the page in the book where it's written.

48

YOU NEED A RAILWAY STATION, A CELLO, YOU NEED
a bassoon, a proper kiss, a choir of starlings
on the roof, shoulder to shoulder, several
instruments, insects, something horizontal,
the woman in the window, gone in a moment,
and the man who passes by and sees her,
doesn't see her, you need the road that's long
as the night, and the Moon, it'll work out, it
sneaks in with the cat, just leave the back door
ajar, a slight draft, and perhaps other creatures
will also find their way, boat refugees, the red
thread, and the child, where did she go? Run
down into the backyard with a ball, you let
the horse pass, wild eyes, sprinkles of froth,
and the rider, not now, they'll have to wait,
you sit at the edge of the field, tear yourself
into tufts of grass, break yourself into twigs,
you need to gather yourself, you'll make it
in a moment or tomorrow, you'll get it done,
and maybe it's not all that important, you think
there's enough time, chances hang in bunches,
bunches on strong trunks with roots growing
deep into the black earth from where the vine
rises, the wine hoisting a flag in your blood,
are you standing on a beach, is the ocean rising
up alongside, is the bedsheet a piece of paper,
is the dream writing you down? But remember
the railway station, freight cars, entrances, exits;
caress is a good word, kayak, spirit level, you need
to pay, you always need something, you want to
give it all away, repay your debt to the earth that
nourishes the tree now giving its life for a poem.

ABRUPTLY AWAKENED BY A COLOUR'S NOISE, DENSE, FURIOUS
mustard, fifteen seconds later the storm breaks loose.
The characters are cut out, a dagger, a single mother,
the word hogweed, having nothing to do with one another,
push in, flash lightning in white light. Lorca had
a dagger and the open sea. In what poem does the word
hogweed appear? And the single mother? Her lover
sings in the shower. I put down the dagger.
Hogweed grows wild in the ditch of a distant
childhood. The hurricane rips the maple tree before
my eyes under a twisted sky. Afterwards
I smoke a metaphorical cigarette in bed.

AN ACUTE ROOT CANAL CLOSER TO THE EDGE.
I needn't say any more. No, but I'll give anything,
my soul and everything that I own! November
and rain, a storm is on its way and The End takes
the shape of a figure standing in the hallway,
scraping and sighing impatiently, a husband
who won't wait for me to correct my lipstick;
the taxi is idling at the gate, honking.
Warm up my pearls, dear, make yourself useful!
A day like today, may it not end so soon.
The earth glistens, fat and heavy, let it wait
in November's rain, let my pearls cast a gentle
melancholy on the evening's little get-together
of shadows and reflections and let this shred
of an opus lie on the table until tomorrow, then
I'll finish it, I promise, and it'll be beautiful!

AFTERWORD
Notes on a Collection of Poems Considered at a Distance

I write poetry for roughly the same reason that I donate blood. I want to give something of myself back to life—as a thank you! Blood is anonymous; letters of the alphabet are, too. I hope my poems are, as well; that is, I hope they are open forms that the reader can find some of his or her own life in, that she or he can settle into them and not feel like a stranger, but like someone long awaited, welcomed and recognized, and be given something useful—new thoughts, diversion, distraction, reflection. Solace. I believe that art can have the same effect on the viewer or the reader as a blood transfusion. When a work of art or a poem *works* there is no need for someone to mediate between the work and the spectator, the poem and the reader; the poem shouldn't need a messenger, an interpreter or intermediary; it must stand on its own. The poet must remove herself from the poem; the poet as a person is insignificant. Of course, you must sense that an actual human being has written the poem; there must be some human presence within the poem. After a donation the body immediately starts producing new blood. Even though my blood type is rather uncommon, in fact, *because* it is uncommon, there is a need for exactly this type of blood. I hope there is also a need for my *type* of poetry. Nothing but blood can replace blood. Whether poems generate more poems the way the body generates new blood is more doubtful—one can always hope—but here we touch upon the domain of inspiration and there are no guarantees. Art, I like to think, is within the world the way blood is within the body: simultaneously a precondition and an outcome.

Do I write in a minor key? Art helps us explore our existence and our human condition. Poetry is primary research. This holds for both the reading and the writing of poetry. In this regard melancholia can be a fine instrument, a resonator. Melancholia has a wide spectrum of nuances and tones and it often evokes a heightened sensitivity. Melancholia is certainly not a negative thing, whereas depression is, and they are not the same. I will forever defend melancholia; it has an inherent power to sharpen certain senses that are beneficial to art, to life.

I have a quite tenuous hold on what is popularly termed reality. Nor am I totally at ease with society. Indeed, with society the thread gets even thinner. I try not to put myself outside, or beside it, but in a way I was born a "fringer" (it sounds friendlier than "outsider") and I live on the "outskirts," as though in a border area; there are refugees, asylum seekers, strays and wanderers; shady transactions take place. It is the osmotic in-between zone, where various solutions glide into one another, I am merely the membrane, I am still not quite sure precisely what my function is. I keep searching. In my poems I attempt to write myself into a community, to give myself (to) a community, but the fact that I write poetry in some way puts me outside any community. Or rather: it estranges me from the idea of community. I peek through the cracks. Take notes.

There is a term in biology, *autotomy*. It is the ability of some animals to shed a limb in a kind of self-amputation (with the aim of self-preservation). Often the discarded limb lies there, twisting and turning so that the animal can elude a predator's grasp or exploit the confusion of its enemy to escape. Lizards, for example, have this ability, as do daddy-long-legs, starfish, crabs and harvest spiders. The poet sheds a poem, leaves it turning on the paper, the page, sheds a whole collection and exploits the confusion to run off! It would be just fine with me if the world were satisfied with my pushing a poem out from under the door of my Hermit crab abode and if it would otherwise leave me to myself. Yes, just fine!

When the manuscript of *Frayed Opus for Strings & Wind Instruments* was complete, it struck me that the poems were full of place names. They are just there; creating a backdrop, pinning one poem here and another one there. I don't attribute any significant or essential meaning to them.

They are just there, not as set pieces, but rather as part of a scenario, as landscapes. The world is specific, concrete. Existence is. I am not good at inventing and I hold on, at a deep level, to a Romantic idea of truth. The fact that I force myself to tell *the truth* requires that I use the actual locations where the poems take place or were conceived, or that I pin a specific moment or event on to a specific place. The place doesn't *mean* anything in itself. The reader can apply his or her own metaphoric meanings, sentiments, interpretations, to a place. Or not. I write the places into the poems as documentary images, backgrounds, motivations. Perhaps they can be read as *states of mind* but even so the places are dependent on the reader's own associations.

Language is the most intimate thing we have, sometimes it terrifies me. Our bodies are publicly accessible; they are in use, for use, in constant decline. Our sexes are merely interesting in glimpses, arranged and subordinated as we are, registered, positioned, aged or aging and in a variety of marital statuses; but in language we show who we are. Language reveals us, exposes us. In language we surrender to the world, even when we try not to or when we try to hide behind language. Even our silences speak. Language is personal common property, an elaborate system of quotes. You cannot invent or add new meanings and values to words all by yourself. Language is a net we throw and capture each other in or that we get caught in ourselves. Language is merciless. We kneel in the dirt and beg for words.

Perhaps it sounds pretentious, or like a conscious experiment, to say that I have tried to broaden my poetic vocabulary. I have been surprised at being able to use words in this collection of poems that I've never used before: lots of food stuffs, lots of place names, lots of details about everyday living. Life is a lot of ordinary everyday living, repetition, lots of specific locations and actions. The street, the backyard, the kiosk, the stairwell, the subway; the putting on the kettle, the at once reassuring and deeply disquieting surrealism of the everyday; that enormous Monday morning steam engine pushed to start up and kept going all the way to Sunday night with stops at every station, every tiny whistle stop, whether you want it or not. It is actually quite reassuring and in a way it has been liberating to discover that it is possible to find diamonds in the junk yard, concrete anchors whence you can zoom out into the world and the universe and get hold of the dark matter, too, and the dead twinkling stars in the galaxy, and the Star Dry Cleaners at Ålekistevej 103 and the Brahmaputra River, which runs through that malty Assam tea I drink gallons of every day, and Dogger Bank, which exists, which is hidden somewhere in the North Sea and is among those magical words I heard on the radio as a child. I used to listen to the marine forecast and the morning church service every day. I didn't really go to school, it was all a bit of a mess, but somehow it turned out okay, though I miss the morning service, the marine forecast. They taught me that the world is magical and dangerous. There are so many words and so much weather going on, metaphors all round. You have to be careful. You have to learn to navigate with the words and the silences in between the words, you have to put yourself right with the wind and the world, the subsea sandbanks, the hidden rocks.

Ulrikka S. Gernes, July 2014

ACKNOWLEDGMENTS

Poems from this translation have been published in *The Malahat Review* and *Eleven Eleven*; thanks to the editors of these publications. Thanks also to the Danish Arts Foundation for their kind support of this book.

It has often been said that a good translation is a new original. Having been under the spell of Per Brask and Patrick Friesen's magic touch, I think these poems are much better in English! And the wonder doesn't stop at that; many years ago Don McKay cleared a path to Brick Books and at the end of that path, like a treasure in the forest, Kitty Lewis was waiting with a warm embrace. I also owe my heartfelt thanks to Jan Zwicky, Alayna Munce, Marijke Friesen, Christopher Haanes. With these people—their skills, hard work, attention and accuracy firmly anchored into each single page—I felt my images, sentences, commas and semicolons to be in safe hands and deeply cared for despite the time difference, the distance, the oceans, and the snow-capped mountain ranges that were between us in the process of making this a book. Not lost—found in translation. Thank you all!

AUTHOR

ULRIKKA S. GERNES was born in 1965 in Sweden to Danish parents.
At the age of twenty-two she moved to Copenhagen, Denmark, already
a published and highly acclaimed poet. Her first collection, *Natsværmer
(Moth)*, was published in Denmark in 1984, when she was eighteen years
old. Since then she has published an additional ten collections, all of them
received gratefully in the Danish press. She is also the author of two books
for children, as well as many short stories, songs, and various contributions
to literary anthologies, art catalogues, magazines, newspapers and Danish
National radio.

In 2001 *A Sudden Sky: Selected Poems*, translated into English by Per
Brask and Patrick Friesen, was published by Brick Books. Over the decades,
poetry has put her on several flights across the Atlantic ocean to read at
festivals in Canada and has also sent her on missions to numerous other
locations across the planet. She manages the estate and artistic legacy of
her father, the internationally known visual artist Poul Gernes, and lives
in Copenhagen, Denmark with her daughter Perle.

TRANSLATORS

PATRICK FRIESEN is a poet, essayist, playwright and translator living in Victoria, B.C. His most recent publications are *jumping in the asylum* (Quattro Books, 2011), *a dark boat* (Anvil Press, 2012) and *a short history of crazy bone* (Mother Tongue Publishing, 2015). He has co-translated five volumes of poetry with Per Brask.

PER BRASK is a Professor in the Department of Theatre and Film at the University of Winnipeg where he has taught since 1982. He has published poetry, short stories, drama, translations, interviews and essays in a wide variety of journals and books. This is his fifth volume of poetry co-translated with Patrick Friesen.